The Freelancer's Handbook

Pursue Your Passion and Profit

Table of Contents

Chapter 1. Introduction

In a world increasingly appreciating the freedom and flexibility of forging one's own career path, 'The Freelancer's Handbook: Pursue Your Passion and Profit' comes as a beacon of brilliance. This Special Report is a dynamic fusion of the exciting world of freelancing and the practicality of turning passion into a tangible source of income. If you have ever dreamed of escaping the 9-5 grind and pursuing what truly speaks to your heart, while also keeping your finances secure, this guide is vital for you. Seamlessly injecting fun into the seriousness of business planning, finance management, and marketplace navigation, this report is your cheerleader and coach in one vibrant, engaging package. So, are you ready to make the leap into a life of creative control and financial prosperity? Our guide is the key to unlocking your freelance potential.

Chapter 2. Discovering Your Passion: A Self-Exploration Journey

Before diving into the exhilarating and, at times, challenging world of freelancing, it is crucial to undergo a thorough process of self-analysis. Figuring out your passions forms the first and most exciting part of this expedition – an expedition to the soul's delight. As the eminent philosopher Confucius once said, "Choose a job you love, and you will never have to work a day in your life."

2.1. The Importance of Self-Exploration

Self-exploration is not merely a whimsical indulgence but an essential process that aids in aligning our skills, desires, and opportunities. For freelancers, this alignment is the bedrock of a fulfilling and profitable venture. To tap into your freelance power means delving into your heart's abyss and verbalizing those genuine interests that ignite your spirit.

2.2. Identifying Your Core Interests

Begin your journey of discovery by penning down your interests. A useful tip is to recollect your youth's fantasies, aspirations, and strong inclinations. Also, think about the activities that give you joy or where you lose track of time.

Make a list of these interests, no matter how varied or unrelated they may seem. Your list item could be based on activities like writing, blogging, coding, photography, graphic designing, cooking, teaching, yoga, musical instruments, or any other activities. This list is the start of your self-exploration journey. At this point, don't worry about monetizing these passions...yet.

2.3. Filtering your List Based on Skills

The next step in this self-exploration journey is to superimpose your skills with your interests. Consider the following questions:

1. In which of these areas are you highly skilled?

2. Are there any areas where you lack skills but are willing to learn?

To make this step more methodical, mark down in front of each passion your current level of proficiency in the skills that form the crux of that activity.

2.4. Matching Passions with Market Demand

Freelancing marries passion with profit. The next step is to examine how your skills fit with market needs. Research extensively on the market demand for your skills. Successful freelancing lies in niches that are a marriage of your skill, passion, and market demand.

Run an online search for freelancing jobs based on your shortlisted skills or use freelancing platforms like Upwork or Fiverr. Look for trends and see which skills are high in demand and in which specific sectors. While topping up your skillset might be an exciting idea, sticking with your natural inclinations and talents will make your passion-based entrepreneurial journey more enjoyable.

2.5. Bridging the Gap

You may find there is a gap between your skills and what the market needs. Take note of these gaps and see them as opportunities for learning and growth. Depending on the urgency and importance, you can fast-track or stagger your learning roadmap.

Consider online courses and certifications on platforms like Coursera, Udemy, Skillshare, or LinkedIn Learning to boost your skillset and stay relevant with changing market dynamics. Nothing goes to waste and every skill learnt will come handy someday!

2.6. Embracing Challenges

The journey of self-exploration and turning passion into a profitable freelancing career is filled with challenges. Embrace them with an open mind and see them as opportunities for self-improvement. It's through overcoming these challenges that you will become a seasoned and successful freelancer. Feel free to revisit the stages in this chapter as self-exploration is an ongoing journey.

Remember, this expedition of soul-searching is not about uncovering the 'right' passion (and there rarely is one single right passion). It's more about revealing a practical synthesis of your passions, skills and market opportunities where you can exercise imaginative control and monetary success.

By going through this journey, you will emerge with a clearer understanding of where your passion lies and how to monetize it through freelancing - thereby setting a strong foundation for your future freelance career.

Chapter 3. Setting the Stage: Creating a Freelancing Plan

Before you can immerse yourself in the passion-fueled world of freelancing, it's essential to lay solid groundwork. A comprehensive freelancing plan will be the cornerstone of your venture, aiding you in establishing, acting, and refining your business goal and strategy.

3.1. Crafting Your Freelancing Vision

Start with the end in mind. What would you like your freelance business to look like in a year from now, in five years? Paint a mental image of your success. Are you consistently booking clients? Have you achieved recognition in your industry? Are you meeting your desired income goals? Once you have this vision sketched out, you can begin building a road map to get there.

3.2. Identifying Your Skills and Talents

For your freelance venture to succeed, you need to base it on skills that you excel in. List all your talents, skills, and areas of expertise. Subsequently, match those skills to the services businesses might be seeking. For example, if you excel at writing compelling narratives, consider freelance roles in content creation or copywriting.

3.3. Determining Your Target Market

Who are the people needing your services? Defining your target market with precision helps in focusing your marketing efforts efficiently. To do this, look at the industries you're most familiar with or passionate about. What recurring problems do they face? Are these issues something your skills can address? If your gardening blog boasts a significant following, for instance, you might choose to target small gardening centers or landscaping businesses that need help with online content.

3.4. Setting Your Rates

Pricing your services is a crucial part of your freelancing plan. Consider the value you're bringing to the clients, factor in the expenses you'd incur, and the profit margin you aim to achieve. The result should be a price that reflects the worth of your work. Take your time to research the market rates for your kind of services. Remember, while it's tempting to charge low to attract clients early, doing so may degrade your work's perceived value, and it may become difficult to raise your rates later.

3.5. Building a Portfolio

A portfolio showcases your skills to potential clients. Gather the best examples of your work to serve as samples. If you're new to the area you're freelancing in, consider doing volunteer work in exchange for testimonials or create samples on your own to demonstrate your skills. Having tangible proof of what you can do goes a long way in convincing clients to hire you.

3.6. Marketing Yourself

Design a strong marketing strategy. Consider who your clients are, where they can be reached, and how to communicate your services effectively. For example, if your target market is online businesses, having a professional website and a sturdy online presence is vital. Use social media platforms, a well-optimized blog, and professional networks for attention. If your market is local businesses, consider networking events, local advertisements, and word-of-mouth referrals as part of your plan.

3.7. Setting Business Goals

Break down your freelancing vision into quantifiable goals. These should be SMART - Specific, Measurable, Attainable, Relevant, and Time-bound. For instance, if your vision includes making a certain income after a year, break down that income into monthly or weekly goals, and then figure out what you need to do to achieve those targets.

3.8. Handling Finances

A financial plan is integral to your freelancing venture's success. It should budget for software, hardware, marketing, taxes, insurance, and more while ensuring a profit margin. Build a solid understanding of your business's financial health by consistently tracking income, expenses, and savings. It is also worthwhile to set aside an emergency fund to handle dry periods in your freelancing business.

3.9. Continual Learning

Freelancing involves wearing many hats; thus, it necessitates an ever-growing skillset. Dedicate time for continual learning and consider investment in courses, books, seminars, and training to stay updated with industry trends and advancements.

Embarking on a freelancing career can be an exhilarating journey. The freedom to choose and chase your projects can bring immense job satisfaction. However, as with any venture, success in freelancing requires careful planning and consistent effort. A well-laid out freelancing plan can serve as the foundation of a fulfilling and profitable freelance career. Therefore, take time now to set your stage right; your future freelance-self will thank you.

Chapter 4. Turning Passion into Skill: Continuous Learning and Improvement

Turning passion into skill is a dynamic process that's achievable by anyone willing to embark on the journey of continuous learning and improvement. Improving oneself takes more than just dedication – it requires the ability to adapt and an unwavering commitment to mastering your craft.

4.1. The Foundation: Defining Your Passion

Before you can become proficient in any field, you need to understand the nature of your passion. What truly drives you? Identifying and defining the thing you love most is the first cornerstone for your foundation for continuous learning and self-improvement. Reflect on your interests and determine what, in particular, lures you in those fields. It's imperative to be specific: it's not enough to be passionate about sports – identify if you're more inclined towards event organization, coaching, sports journalism, or even equipment design.

4.2. Setting Clear Goals: What Does Improvement Look Like to You?

Setting goals allows you to measure progress and provides direction for your learning pathway. Start by formulating a goal statement that defines where you want to be. Be clear, specific, and realistic. Aim for an objective you can measure to track your progression over time, such as "Improving my writing speed from 500 words per hour to 800 words per hour within a span of two months."

4.3. Crafting a Learning Path: Create a Roadmap for Success

Once you've defined your passion and set clear goals, it's time to map out a learning pathway that will enable you to transform your passion into a tangible skill. There are numerous routes to take, so adapt your path based on your learning style, available resources, and time commitments. The pathway may include attending workshops, undertaking online courses, finding a mentor, or self-learning through books.

4.4. Lifelong Learning: The Key to Adaptation and Growth

Lifelong learning forms the backbone of continuous improvement. You need to keep refining your skills, acquiring new knowledge, and staying up-to-date with current trends. Join online forums, subscribe to newsletters, stay active in relevant communities, and set aside time for learning. Lifelong learning isn't an obligation; it's a habit that fuels personal and professional growth.

4.5. Embracing Failure: Your Teacher in Disguise

Failure isn't a signal of incompetence; it's part of the learning process. It provides invaluable lessons that pave the way for future success. Embrace each failure, reflect on what went wrong, make the necessary adjustments, and then proceed with modified strategies.

4.6. Building a Portfolio: Showcasing Your Progress and Skills

A portfolio is a visual representation of your learning journey, illustrating your progress and capabilities. It is an ever-evolving platform in which you can showcase your work, demonstrate your experience, and highlight your accomplishments. A well-structured portfolio can be an influential tool when seeking clients or establishing a professional presence in your field.

4.7. Constructive Criticism and Feedback: Opportunity for Refinement

Feedback is an excellent tool for self-improvement. It can illuminate areas of strength and highlight places where you require more practice or adjustments. Strive to seek constructive criticism from experienced individuals within your field to gain insight into possible improvements. Also, assess your work personally to recognize weaknesses and turn them into strengths.

4.8. The Power of Patience: Progress Takes Time

Remember, honing your skills won't be an overnight process. Turning passion into skill requires time, patience, and relentless determination. Celebrate each small victory and use it as motivation to push through. The journey itself is just as, if not more, valuable than the destination.

4.9. Recap and Future Directions

Following your passion and committing to continuous learning and improvement can lead to a fulfilling freelance career. This journey may be challenging, requiring hard work, patience, and resilience, but it is undeniably rewarding in personal and financial freedom.

Taking these steps towards improvement doesn't mark the end of your journey but the start of a new phase. As you transition from learning to freelancing, you'll inevitably encounter new objectives and undertake an additional round of goal setting, learning, and adaptation.

In the world of freelancing, the only constant is change, and the ability to adapt and evolve is essential. Now equipped with the knowledge of how to convert your passion into a marketable skill and remain committed to continuous learning and improvement, you're ready for the exciting journey ahead. It's time to step outside your comfort zone and embrace the infinite possibilities inherent in your passion.

Chapter 5. Business Basics: Understanding Finances and Legalities

Understanding finances, legalities, and business basics may sound intimidating, but it's absolutely essential for your success as a freelancer. It's all about dressing for the job you want, not the job you have, and being as professional as possible in your own business operations. So let's break down these complex topics into some manageable sub-sections.

5.1. Financial Management: The Freelancer's Lifeline

Your financial management skills directly tie into your ability to keep the job you love. Here's what you need to know:

Income Evaluation: As a freelancer, your income may vary. You must develop a habit of periodically evaluating your income from different projects or sources.

1. What were your earnings this month?

2. How does this month compare to the last?

3. What changes can you see, and what influenced them?

This process will contribute significantly to your income stability over time.

Budgeting: A well-thought-out budget is indispensable. The general guideline is to divide expenses into 'Needs', 'Wants', and 'Savings'. A disciplined approach to budgeting will cushion you against potential income variability.

Debt Management: As a freelancer, having financial freedom is crucial. You need to have a plan regarding your loan repayments and endeavor to remain debt-free as much as possible.

Emergency Funds: It's essential to have a financial safety net. An emergency fund that can sustain you for 3-6 months of expenses is a good start.

5.2. Understanding Taxes: The Good Citizen's Duty

Tax law varies greatly, so the below information is quite general. You may need a tax advisor to get advice tailored specifically for you.

Tax Deductions: As a freelancer, it's crucial to understand what expenses you can write off against your income. Typical examples may include your home office, travel expenses, or even your internet bill.

Estimated Taxes: Most freelancers are required to pay estimated taxes quarterly. These are simply payments you make to cover your income tax, self-employment tax, and potentially your estimated deductible expenses.

Keeping Records: Record keeping is vital. Ensure to keep track of your business receipts, invoices, and statements. This will simplify your taxes and potentially result in major savings when tax time rolls around.

5.3. Legal Basics: Covering your Assets

Let's delve into some simple legal basics every freelancer should be aware of:

Contracts: A well-drafted contract protects you in case of a dispute between you and your clients. The contract should have clear terms covering the project scope, payment terms, confidentiality clauses, and contract termination conditions.

Intellectual Property: This refers to creations of the mind for which exclusive rights are recognized. Protecting your intellectual property is critical in the marketplace.

Business Structure: Determining whether to operate as a sole proprietor, partnership, limited liability company, or corporation will have substantial tax and liability implications. Consult a business advisor before deciding on your structure.

Licenses and Permits: Depending on your locality or the nature of your business, you may need specific licenses or permits to operate legally. Check local and federal requirements.

5.4. The Wrap Up: What have we learned?

In this chapter, we learned about financial management essentials, including income evaluation and budgeting; the importance of understanding taxes, keeping records, and seeking out deductions where possible; and finally, key legal principles protecting our business.

With these tools in your toolbox, you'll be in a solid position to navigate the financial and legal landscape that often intimidates those newer to freelancing. Remember to revisit and review these sections as you evolve in your freelancing journey, and never hesitate to reach out to professionals for detailed help.

Chapter 6. Creating Your Freelance Brand: Marketing and Positioning

As a freelancer setting out on a new path, the first critical step you'll need to take is creating your brand. A brand is a promise; it's what clients can expect when they work with you, and it's the distinctive personality and values that separate you from the competition. In order to create a successful freelance brand, you'll need to master the art of marketing and positioning.

6.1. What is Your Brand?

Think of your brand as an external representation of your work ethic, skills, experiences, and personality. It will be the identity that you'll market to your prospective clients. By shaping your brand, potential clients can quickly form an understanding of who you are and what you offer even before they interact with you.

Take time to deliberate on your core values, strengths, and what sets your offering apart. Are you an SEO wizard who guarantees organic traffic growth? Are you a graphic designer who specializes in minimalistic designs? Alternatively, do you excel at creating engaging blog content that captivates audiences?

Itemize your unique attributes and how these meet the needs of a specific market. Define this in clear terms, and embed it in all your professional communications - your website, portfolio, and social media platforms - to project a unified brand message.

6.2. Understanding Marketing

Marketing is a vast field, and familiarity with its primary principles is useful in positioning your brand effectively. To simplify, marketing lies in "creating value" and "communicating value."

1. Creating value pertains to understanding your clients' needs and rendering services that fulfill those needs. It may also involve going over and above expectations to deliver satisfactory results.

2. "Communicating value" involves showcasing your value to your target audience. This can be done through various channels such as social media, networking events, or your professional website.

Remember, 'out of sight is out of mind.' Regular and effective communication keeps your brand at the forefront of potential clients' minds when they need your services.

6.3. Positioning Your Brand

Positioning is determining where you fit in the marketplace vis-a-vis your competitors. Other freelancers might offer similar services, but your unique value proposition (UVP) sets you apart.

Start positioning your brand by identifying who your ideal client is. What industry are they in? What is their budget? What kind of work will they need? Once you have identified these, it becomes easier to tailor your services to this demography.

Carve your niche by reflecting on what you do best and what you enjoy doing. Find or create a space within your market where these intersect. That's your sweet spot, and it's where you should position your brand.

6.4. Building Your Portfolio

Your portfolio is your brand's visual representation. It's where potential clients can view your past work, acquire an understanding of your competence and skills, and determine if your style aligns with their needs. Your portfolio should contain your best work and updated frequently to reflect evolving competencies and trends. Be sure to solicit testimonials from satisfied clients, as this adds credibility to your brand.

6.5. Showcasing Your Brand Online

Your online presence is key to reaching potential clients. A professional website and active social media profiles can offer an easy way for clients to reach out and trust your services.

Ensure these platforms align with your brand's tone and voice. For instance, if your brand is playful and artistic, a formally toned website will create dissonance. Consider investing in professional website design and SEO to boost online visibility.

6.6. Networking

Networking, both online and offline, should be an integral part of your marketing strategy. Freelance job platforms, industry-specific message boards, LinkedIn groups, and local business events can present networking opportunities.

Remember to always have your business cards handy. Additionally, each interaction presents an opportunity to mention your freelancing services subtly. Over time, this helps to make both you and your brand known in your industry and beyond.

Effective branding, along with proper marketing and positioning, is essential for any successful freelance business. They ensure you attract the right clients, boosts your visibility, and enhances your professional reputation. Make sure to take some time to build a brand that truly represents you and your unique business offering. It may very well be the bedrock upon which your long-term freelance success is built.

Chapter 7. Toolkit for Success: Essential Tools and Platforms for Freelancers

In the realm of freelancing, your choice of tools as well as the platform you will utilize significantly impacts your productivity and success. When you have the right tools at your disposal, you amplify your efficiency, boost your visibility, and generally make your job a whole lot easier. Let's explore these essential tools and platforms in detail.

7.1. Navigating the Technical Landscape

As a freelancer, it's vital that you become comfortable with using a variety of digital tools. What's most significant is identifying the tools that match your particular needs and learning how to utilize them efficiently.

7.1.1. Organizational and Time Management Tools

Managing your time effectively is crucial in freelancing. Thankfully, numerous tools can make your scheduling quicker and less prone to errors.

1. **Google Calendar:** This versatile tool syncs seamlessly across different devices, letting you manage your time precisely wherever you are. It can update in real time, allowing clients to see your availability, making booking appointments a breeze.

2. **Trello:** This is another powerful tool for organization, allowing you to manage projects, set deadlines, and track progress all from

a visually pleasing interface.

3. **Asana:** If you're collaborating with others, Asana is a great choice. This tool offers sleek task and project management with team integration features.

7.1.2. Communication Tools

A fruitful freelancing career relies greatly on effective communication. Here are some tools to simplify the process:

1. **Zoom:** A video conferencing tool that became tremendously useful during the pandemic, Zoom is great for video meetings and presentations.

2. **Slack:** Designed as a team collaboration tool, Slack can be used for direct messaging, group chats, and integrations with other productivity tools.

3. **WhatsApp:** This application is straightforward and versatile, supporting text chats, video, and audio calls, offering a less formal communication medium.

7.2. Harnessing the Power of Social Media

Social media is a freelancer's best friend for networking and showcasing work. Platforms can serve as a digital portfolio, as well as an avenue for finding or attracting potential clients.

7.2.1. LinkedIn

LinkedIn has become the go-to medium for professional networking. Having an updated LinkedIn profile with your latest projects and skills can attract potential clients to your services. Engaging with posts and joining relevant groups can also generate leads and partnerships.

7.2.2. Instagram

If your freelance work involves visual and creative components like graphic design, photography, or content creation, Instagram can be a powerful platform to showcase your portfolio. Make sure to use appropriate tags for increased visibility.

7.2.3. Twitter

Twitter is excellent for engaging with others in your industry. Participating in discussions, and posting useful, thoughtful content can position you as a thought leader in your field, attracting high-value clients.

7.3. Leveraging Freelance Marketplaces

These platforms have surfaced as hotspots for freelancers to network, exhibit their skills, and land prospective gigs.

7.3.1. Upwork

One of the largest freelance platforms, Upwork caters to a wide range of professions. Having a comprehensive, well-crafted profile can help you attract clients on this platform.

7.3.2. Fiverr

With a unique structure where freelancers post the services they offer, Fiverr has attracted many freelancers and clients alike. It's easy to set up and offers a great way to kickstart your freelance venture.

7.3.3. Freelancer

Freelancer is an extensive marketplace with millions of projects. As a freelancer, you can bid on a range of projects matching your skill set.

7.4. Essential Tools for Finance Management

Proper finance management can be the difference between a successful freelance career and a struggling one.

7.4.1. FreshBooks

FreshBooks is a software designed for small businesses that simplifies invoicing, time tracking, and expense management. It helps freelancers manage finances without being financial experts themselves.

7.4.2. QuickBooks

A comprehensive tool for managing finances, QuickBooks allow freelancers to track expenses, invoice clients, and even calculate and pay taxes.

7.4.3. Paypal

PayPal is not only a universal online payment platform but also offers functions including invoicing and expense tracking.

This comprehensive list is by no means exhaustive. Consider this as an initial guide to assist you in establishing your freelancing toolkit. As your freelance career evolves, your toolkit will too. Remember, the most crucial aspect is to choose the tools and platforms that suit your requirements best. With the right systems in place, your freelancing career will flourish without the limitations or restrictions of conventional 9-5 jobs. So, embrace the freedom of freelancing and materialize your dreams into reality.

Chapter 8. Networking for Freelancers: Building Connections that Matter

In the highly competitive and creative world of freelancing, establishing a diverse and robust professional network is not just beneficial – it's essential. Possessing the right skills and offering competitive pricing are elements of success, but they aren't sufficient. Building meaningful connections will help you stand out in a saturated market, secure more fruitful opportunities, and foster long-term relationships.

8.1. Importance of Networking in Freelancing

Networking is not merely the act of exchanging business cards or connecting on professional platforms like LinkedIn. It's about building meaningful relationships that can catapult your freelancing career to new heights.

- It opens doors to new opportunities: Networking allows you to meet potential clients, partners and mentors. These connections can lead to job opportunities, collaborations, partnerships, or merely a chance to learn from someone who's been there.

- It propels word-of-mouth marketing: A significant amount of freelancing work is secured through referrals. When people in your network speak positively about your work to others, they do more than just recommending – they endorse you.

- It offers fresh perspectives: Networking can offer new insights into your field and potential market trends. It can keep you updated, inspire you with fresh ideas, and even help you avoid pitfalls.

8.2. Building a Network from Scratch

Knowing the importance of networking is one thing, but how to build a network from scratch is another. Here's how you can start:

- Identify your target audience: Gain clarity on the type of people you need in your network. These could be potential clients, industry peers, mentors, industry influencers, or potential collaborators.

- Prioritize quality over quantity: Choose deep over broad. A smaller network of influential people who genuinely appreciate your work is far more helpful than a large network of weak ties.

- Be genuine: Authenticity is key in networking. People appreciate genuine interest and connection over someone who only builds connections for personal gain.

8.3. Effectively Utilizing Online Platforms

In the digital age, several online platforms can help you build and nurture your professional network.

- Social media platforms: LinkedIn is a quintessential platform for your professional networking efforts. Additionally, platforms like Facebook, Instagram, and Twitter enable you to showcases your personality alongside your work.

- Freelancer forums and websites: Websites like Upwork or forums like Reddit can offer plenty of networking opportunities. Join discussions, ask questions, and show your willingness to help others.

- Attend virtual meetups and webinars: Such events are vital sources of networking. They present the opportunity to meet like-minded professionals and industry experts.

8.4. Offline Networking Opportunities

While online networking is influential, it doesn't entirely replace the value of meeting in person.

- Join local meetups and networking events: These are perfect platforms to interact with potential clients and other freelancers.

- Attend conferences and seminars: They offer an excellent opportunity to meet industry leaders, learn new skills, and stay updated with industry trends.

8.5. Maintaining and Nurturing Your Network

Building your network is just half the battle won. To reap the benefits, you must maintain and nurture your relationships.

- Regular communication: Keep in touch with your contacts regularly. Send a friendly note, share valuable information, or just catch up over coffee.

- Reciprocate: Do not just take; give back. Offer your help when your contacts need it, endorse their work, or refer them to potential opportunities.

In conclusion, networking is a vital arsenal in a freelancer's tool kit. It opens up new horizons and helps establish a lasting reputation in your sector. Successfully building and fostering relationships can set the tone for a prosperous, fulfilling freelancing journey. Yes, it takes time and effort, but remember - "Your network is your net worth."

Chapter 9. Dealing with Challenges: Coping Strategies for Freelancers

Taking the leap into freelancing can be exhilarating, yet fraught with challenges. The road to freelance success is not always a smooth one. It's lined with obstacles, bends, and roadblocks that can awaken doubts and fears. But fret not, as a freelancer, these challenges often become catalysts for personal growth and reinvention.

9.1. Understanding the Challenges of Freelancing

The first step in coping with challenges is understanding the nature of these hurdles. Some common problems that freelancers face include finding clients, loneliness, managing finances, and the instability of freelance work.

1. Finding clients: Perhaps the most significant challenge new freelancers face is drumming up business. It can be tough to convince potential clients that you're the right person for the job when you're just starting and lack a body of work or references.

2. Loneliness: Freelancing can be isolating. You'll often find yourself working hours on end without interacting with anyone. This lack of social connection can be mentally exhausting.

3. Managing finances: Money management is a perennial issue for freelancers. Without a steady paycheck, you'll need to strategically budget and plan your finances to avoid dry spells.

4. The instability of freelance work: One month, you might have more work than you can handle, and the next month, you might have nothing. This unpredictability can induce stress and

uncertainty about maintaining a consistent income.

9.2. Coping Strategies for Freelancers

Now that you have an overview of some of the significant challenges that freelancers face, let's explore some coping strategies that lead to success in the tumultuous world of freelancing.

1. Building a Robust Network: Networking can solve or at least mitigate the problem of finding clients. Start by reaching out to your immediate contacts, attend industry-specific events, webinars, and leverage platforms like LinkedIn and Twitter. Remember, networking is not about directly selling your services, but about creating relationships that can yield client referrals over time.

2. Creating a Comfortable Workspace: Working from home can be isolating, but setting up a comfortable and motivating workspace can help. Surround your work area with things you love, like plants, inspiring quotes, or pictures of loved ones.

3. Forming a Freelancer's Group: You can join meetups or forums of freelancers in your area or online. Apart from finding companionship, you can exchange tips, industry knowledge, and possibly collaborate on larger projects together.

4. Smart Financial Planning: Discipline in managing your finances is critical. Set up a budget and stick to it. Emergency funds can cover up to six months of living expenses in case you face income instability. It is also advisable to take a course or hire a financial advisor to help you navigate freelancers' unique financial landscape.

5. Diversification of Clients: To mitigate income instability, it's wise not to rely on a single client. Try to strike a balance between having enough clients to ensure financial security, but not so

many that you are swamped with work.

6. Prioritizing Health: Stress, isolation, and long work hours can take a toll on your physical and mental health. Ensure you are setting aside time each day to exercise, eat healthily, and have social interactions outside of work.

7. Upskilling Regularly: The marketplace is dynamic, and new tools and techniques are constantly emerging. Regular upskilling ensures that you stay relevant and appealing to potential clients.

8. Defining Work Boundaries: Saying no is important. It's tempting to take on every task that comes your way, but this can quickly lead to burnout. Understand your limits, and don't be afraid to turn down work if you're already at capacity.

Remember, challenges are inherent to the freelance journey, but they can be adequately managed with a good set of coping strategies in place. As you navigate your freelance career, keep adapting these strategies. You'll discover what works best for you and uncover new ways to stay resilient and profitable as a freelancer long term.

Chapter 10. Sustaining the Freelance Life: Long-term Strategies and Growth

As a freelancer, your life is never stagnant. Through a wave of thriving success and occasional periods of drought, maintaining your momentum and nurturing growth is crucial. Let's look at some key strategies to sustain this entrepreneurial commitment and explore how to facilitate long-term growth.

10.1. Budgeting and Financial Planning

Freelancing often comes with fluctuating income streams, making budgeting and financial planning a vital aspect of running a successful freelance business.

Firstly, it helps to monitor your income and expenses. To handle your uncertain income, financial advisors often recommend following a 'zero-based budgeting' system where each dollar has a purpose before you receive it. It can help you operate within your means and provide financial discipline.

Furthermore, establish an emergency fund that covers at least six months of living expenses. Unanticipated circumstances can arise at any time, and without steady income, these situations can become particularly stressful. If you can build a financial safety net, times of crisis can turn into bumps on the road instead of complete roadblocks.

Regularly review your rates, making necessary adjustments to reflect market trends, your expanding skills, and rising living costs.

However, consider your clients' perspectives and be justifiable with your raises.

Lastly, consider consulting with a financial advisor or an accountant to help manage your freelance finance and taxes. An expert opinion can often ward off potential financial blunders and help outline strategies to maximize your cash flow.

10.2. Marketing and Brand Development

Marketing can be overwhelming, but it's essentially a way to tell your story and share your work. Effective marketing ensures a steady influx of clients, vital for freelance stability.

Start by defining your brand. Your brand is your identity. It reflects your unique selling propositions, your values, and your skills. Making your brand resonate with potential clients can greatly influence your success.

However, marketing isn't a one-and-done deal. It should be ongoing, with regular updates to your website and portfolio. Regular blogging can help you create an authoritative voice in your field while social media networking can help you reach broader audiences.

When it comes to marketing, consistency is key. Keep the look, feel, and tone of your messages consistent - this includes everything from your website design, your portfolio, down to your email correspondence. A consistent brand is an enduring brand.

10.3. Networking and Collaborations

Networking is essential for freelancer survival. Constructive networking can generate invaluable support from peers and businesses alike.

A simple starting point is joining and actively participating in relevant freelancing and industry-specific forums and associations. They offer platforms to build relationships, learn from others, and gain business insights.

In this digital age, networking isn't restricted to physical interactions. You can also consider LinkedIn groups, Facebook communities and even Twitter chats. Try to establish meaningful interactions, rather than simply focusing on sales.

Collaborations with other freelancers or businesses can also provide a great opportunity for reciprocal growth. You exchange expertise, broaden your client base and add variety to your portfolio.

10.4. Skill Diversification and Professional Development

In freelancing, your skills are your assets. But markets and trends are continually changing, which requires constant learning and professional development.

Focus on diversification in your skills without losing your specialization. Adding complementary skills to your portfolio can make you "hard to replace" . For instance, a graphic designer may learn motion design or copywriting.

Online platforms like Coursera, Skillshare, LinkedIn Learning, and others, offer courses on a variety of subjects, allowing you to learn at your pace.

10.5. Client Management

Long-term client relationships often form the backbone of successful freelancing. Continuously work on nurturing and strengthening these relationships.

Delivering consistently high-quality work is a given, but think of building relationships beyond transactions. Put forth solid communication structures, listen effectively to their needs and respond timely. Show genuine interest in their business and take hold of opportunities to provide value beyond your service.

Regularly ask for feedback and be proactive in addressing their concerns. This simple practice can bring agility to your services, align your work with client expectations, and prevent potential misunderstandings.

Chapter 11. Embracing Balance

Lastly, remember to accept the ups and downs of the freelance life as part of the journey. There can be periods of high demand, but also quieter times. Consider having diversified client sources to avoid dependency on one client too much.

Remember, your freelance journey is a marathon, not a sprint. Emphasize balance in your work and personal life. Build your routine around what works for you, when you are most productive. Allow time for breaks, relaxation, and any other personal pursuits.

This strategy demands patience, commitment, and resilience. But with these, you'll find yourself well-equipped to weather fluctuations, emerge stronger after setbacks, and enjoy sustainable growth in your freelancing career.

Chapter 12. Balancing Act: Freelancing and Personal Life

Leading a successful freelance life doesn't mean sidelining your personal life. It's crucial to strike the right balance between professional and personal responsibilities to make sure one area does not overshadow the other. Ensure you are crafting a lifestyle that facilitates growth, personal development, and job satisfaction.

12.1. Kicking Off: Understand Freelancing Isn't a 9-5 Job

Freelancing is not your standard office job. It characteristically comes with its own set of benefits and intricacies. The beauty of freelancing is that it offers flexibility and autonomy, but it could also mean that you might be working at unorthodox hours. Acknowledging this fact is the first step towards maintaining a proper work-life balance.

Your work hours might spill into evenings or weekends, and you might often find yourself juggling multiple tasks at the same time. This flexibility, however, also allows you to accommodate your personal commitments effectively. The key to managing this is to maintain a strict schedule and adhering to it.

Remember to pencil in some 'me time' into your schedule. It's crucial to establish boundaries between job responsibilities and personal time to avoid burnout. You have the control over your schedule, so don't plunge into a workaholic state, neglecting your personal life and health.

12.2. Mind the Gap: Navigating Vacant Hours

Unlike a job with scheduled working hours, freelancing can be unpredictable. There may be multiple assignments in a week and then none for a while. The ebb and flow of work will require you to manage your personal life around your work.

It's essential to use your downtime wisely when work is slow. Rather than fretting over a quiet period, use this time to recharge, learn a new skill, network, tend to family, or catch up with friends. These vacant hours can also be leveraged for self-care, such as exercise, pursuing a hobby, or simply relaxing.

12.3. Boundary Setting: Creative Spaces and Personal Spaces

Create a physical demarcation between your workspace and personal space where possible. Having a dedicated workspace signals to your brain that it's time to work and helps you switch to 'work mode.' When you step away from this space, it should symbolize 'logging off' for the day.

Getting caught in the 'one more email' trap is common amongst freelancers, which can lead to a struggle in separating personal and work life. Avoid taking your work to bed or a family dinner table. There should be tangible boundaries between work hours and personal hours.

12.4. Time Off: Vacation Time

Freelancing affords the luxury of taking vacation time at your own discretion. However, the fear of losing out on potential business often dissuades freelancers from making the most of this advantage. Be sure to communicate your plans with your clients in advance, handle your pending tasks, and ensure your clients that you will be available in case of emergencies even during your time off.

Remember, just as your clients deserve your best work, your family and friends deserve your undivided attention during breaks. Work-related stress can affect not only your mental health but can also strain your personal relationships.

12.5. Master the Art of Saying 'No'

Freelancers often end up taking on more than they can handle, thinking they might miss out on future opportunities. Without the constraints of a traditional 9-5 job, it's easy to lose sight of one's bandwidth. But remember, it's okay to turn down projects if they seem to interfere with your personal life or if they don't align with your professional objectives.

12.6. Proper Planning: Financial Stability

It's important to recognise that freelancing is often synonymous with financial unpredictability. To help mitigate this, create a budget planning system. This involves keeping track of your income, expenses, and savings, which contributes to maintaining a stable personal life.

Having an open discussion about finances with your family will also dispel anxieties related to income instability. Knowing you are financially prepared for a break in work will provide reassurance thereby allowing freelancing and personal life to co-exist harmoniously.

Freelancing is not an escape from work; it's an embrace of work on one's own terms. The balancing act between freelancing and personal life is no easy feat, but with careful planning, discipline, and mindfulness, it certainly becomes manageable. It's an exploration of personal and professional potentials that leads to a harmonious co-existence of passion and life enjoyments. Leading a thriving freelance career while keeping personal life in sync is an achievable reality — persevere it.